The Beginners Guide to using a Windows Computer

By: Robert Beers

Booting from another devise on start up

Step 1. Start or restart your computer.

Step 2. You will need to read when the computer starts to find the correct key to push. All computers are different.

Step 3. If you choose the Bios then go to the Boot Options and choose what you want to boot from.

Step 4. If you chose to pick from the quick boot then just pick what you want to boot from.

Warning:

I recommend anyone who does not know anything about computers to choose from the Quick Boot options. Messing around in the bios can destroy your computer.

Starting in safe mode

Safe Mode is a version of windows were nothing is running. You use Safe

Mode when you have a virus that is causing your virus software to not work, or you

can not do a system restore.

Step 1. Start or Restart your computer.

Step 2. To get in to Safe Mode press the F8 key at the top of your keyboard.

Step 3. It will give you options of how you would like to start Safe Mode. You can

run it with Network enabled or disabled.

Speed up your computers start up

If your computer takes forever to boot that may mean that you have to much

starting up. All of the programs that are set to start up when you turn your

computer on eats up RAM and can slow your computer down a lot. Follow these steps to

stop all the unnecessary programs from booting when your computer start.

Step 1. Go down to your start menu button. It is located at the bottom left hand corner.

Step 2. When the start menu opens, look for the Run icon and push it.

Step 3. A window will open with a blank line. In that line you will type msconfig, then push OK.

Step 4. Now the System Configuration Utility window has opened. You will go to the Tab called Start up. You will see a bunch of programs in there, that are checked. Those are the Programs that are starting when windows does.

Step 5. Look through the list of Start Up items. It is safe for you to un-check any program that begins with C:\ProgramFiles\. Just remember that if you are running virus, windows defender, or any other protection software it may begin with Program Files.

Step 6. Un-check any of the Program Files you wish to stop starting up.

Step 7. When you have unchecked the program that you want to stop starting up press OK. It will ask if you would like to restart your computer. You do not have to but it is recommended that you do right away.

Step 8. When your computer restarts the next time, you will get this message "You have changed your Start Up Configurations" Don't be alarmed! All you need to do is check the box that says "Don't show this message or launch System Configurations when windows restarts."

Automatic Windows Updates

It is very important that you have your Automatic Updates activated. Your computer gets critical updates from Microsoft this helps your computers security from attackers. Here are the steps to be sure that it is activated or that you activate it.

Step 1. You will need to go to the Start menu.

Step 2. Once the start menu comes up, look for the link called Control Panels. Click
that.

Step 3. Click on the Security Center link.

Step 4. Look for the link called Automatic Updates. Then click it.

Step 5. Make sure the circle or box next to Automatic is checked. Makes sure it is set to download updates everyday and you pick the time that's best for you.

Step 6. Press OK. Your done setting up your Automatic Updates!

Download Windows Updates Manually

You can also download the updates manually. When you do this you can also update more than just critical updates. You have three options. Critical updates, Hardware, and Software updates. Follow these steps to update your computer manually.

Step 1. Go to WWW.update.Microsoft.com

Step 2. If this is your first time, you may need to install ActiveX. The site will tell you and walk you through how.

Step 3. Once it loads click the button that says Custom. Now it will search your computer for any updates needed.

Step 4. On the left hand side there is 3 choices. High Priority, Software Optional, Hardware Optional. You can install all the updates from them all.

Step 5. Once you have selected all the updates you wish to install, press Review and
Install. You may have to restart your computer after they Install.

Activating Windows Firewall

It is important that you activate your Windows built in Firewall. The firewall helps to protect your computer from Viruses and some attack attempts. Here are steps to be sure your Firewall is active.

Step 1. Go to your Start Menu. Click it.

Step 2. Go to the Control Panel Link. Click on it.

Step 3. Click on the Security Center Icon in Control Panels.

Step 4. Go down to the Icon labeled Windows Firewall. Click that.

Step 5. Check to be sure that the box is checked Next to ON. If not check it.

Step 6. Press OK. You have now activated your Windows Firewall.

Adding or Removing Programs

This is used so you do not have to look for the un-install for a program. You can remove all unused program so that you can clear space for new ones. To use the Adding or Removing programs just follow these steps.

Step 1. Click on your Start Menu.

Step 2. In the Start Menu find and click on Control Panels.

Step 3. When Control Panels opens find the Add or Remove Programs link. Click that.

Step 4. Look through the list of programs. If you see one you want to get rid of then
click it.

Step 5. Now that you have highlighted a program to get rid of look for the Change/Remove Button. Click that.

Step 6. Repeat steps 4 and 5 until you are done. Now Restart your computer and your done.

Disk Cleanup

Disk Cleanups main purpose it to clean the temporary files that your computer saves. It can also empty your recycling bin for you if you haven't done so. These steps will walk you through on how to use the Disk Cleanup.

Step 1. You will need to find your My Computer Icon. If it is not on your desktop then you will need to go to you start menu and open it that way or press the windows key + E.

Step 2. Go down to the drive you wish to clean. Most people only clean drive C. Now right Click it.

Step 3. Now a menu should have opened when you right clicked on the drive. Go to

the Properties which should be the last choice.

Step 4. Now a window should have opened. Look at the top it should be in the

General Tab. You should be able to see a Pie Chart, that is your Hard Drive usage. Now look for the Button that says Disk Cleanup. Push that Button.

Step 5. When the window called Disk Cleanup comes up you notice a bunch or stuff

that you can select. Choose what you want to be cleaned up.

Step 6. Once you have selected everything you want to be cleaned press the OK Button and let it erase all that stuff.

Defragging your computer

Though time you have added and deleted stuff from the computer. This causes your files to become Defraged. When I say Defraged I mean it moves pars of files all over the place causing your computer to have to work harder to start programs. When your computer has to work harder it eats up more RAM causing your computer to slow down. I recommend that you Defrag your computer at least once a month or after you do a mass delete of stuff. To run the Defrag program follow these steps.

Step 1. Locate the My Computer Icon. If it is not located on your desktop you will need to go to your Start Menu and open it from there or press the windows key + E.

Step 2. Now that you have opened My Computer you now need to Right Click Drive C, or what ever drive you are trying to Defrag.

Step 3. After Right Clicking you need to go to the option that says Properties Should be the last option.

Step 4. The properties window should have opened. You should be in the general Tab, right next to were it says General you see the Tools Tab Push that.

Step 5. In tools you see 3 options look for the one that says Disk Defragmentor. Click it.

Step 6. The Disk Defragmentor should have opened. Go down to the bottom, you should see two options Analyze and Defragment. You need to pus the Defragment Button.

Step 7. Disk Defraging will take a while to complete. So I Recommend you do this
when you don't need the computer.

Scan Your Disk for Errors

From time to time windows files go corrupt and causes your computer to crash and or slow down. The best thing about that is Microsoft has included a scan disk program in windows. The scan disk program can fix many errors but as everything it can not repair everything. Follow these steps so that you can check your computer for any errors so you can correct them before its to late.

Step 1. You need to find the My Computer Icon. If not on the desktop you will need
to go to your Start Menu and open it that way or you can press the windows
key + E at the same time.

Step 2. Once you open My Computer you will need to go down to the Drive you
would like to check, most likely it will be C. Right click the Drive and go to
properties.

Step 3. You will notice that it opened up in General. You will need to select the
Tools Tab next to General.

Step 4. The first of the 3 options is the one you will select. Before you do check to
be
sure its the Error Checking one. If it is click the button.

Step 5. You have now entered the Error checker you will notice there is 2
unchecked boxes you need to check them both. Once you have check them
press Start.

Step 6. Don't be alarmed when it ask you if you would like to schedule the scan
for
the next time you start Windows. Select yes for that option then press OK.
Restart your computer and let it scan it will take a while.

System Restore

System Restore is used to restore your computer back to an earlier working Stage. You would want to use system restore if you have been having a lot of errors. Just because it restores your computer back to an earlier time doesn't mean it is going to delete your save programs and personal stuff. There are two ways you can access System Restore. Follow these steps.

Step 1. The First way to start system restore is to press F11 when the computer is just starting up when u just turn it on or restart.

Step 2. The Second way to do a System Restore can be done in both Safe Mode and

in a Normal windows boot.

Step 3. In the start menu go to Control Panels.

Step 4. When the Control Panels window opens Press the System and Maintenance

Link.

Step 5. On the left hand side you should see options under See Also that says System Restore. Click the link and follow Restores Directions.

User Accounts

You would use User Accounts to create a new account for someone or to update an existing account. You can add log in passwords for each individual account. You use this to set the user account privileges. It is best to have your administrator account separate from your everyday use account. Only use your administrator account when you are installing new programs, not being in your administrator account helps to prevent viruses from changing your registry files. To locate the User Account menu follow these steps.

Step 1. Click on the Start Menu Button.

Step 2. When the Start Menu opens, find the icon named Control Panels. Click that.

Step 3. Once Control Panels opens, look for the User Account icon. Click that. Now
set up your accounts.

Create a new Folder

You would create a new folder to place documents and other icons you wish to put in a place to keep them organized. Most people create folders on their desktop so that it does not look like a mess. To create a folder follow these steps.

Step 1. Right Click anywhere on your desktop.

Step 2. A set of options will appear. Select the option that says new, it will open a new set of options.

Step 3. In the new set of options that just opened you need to look for the option that says folder. Once you have found that click that option.

Step 4. A new folder should have appeared on your desktop. If the name is highlighted push the delete key or Backspace and type in the new name you wish to call it. If it is not highlighted please refer to step 5.

Step 5. Use this Step if your folder is highlighted or you wish to rename another file
then you will need to right click the file and go to the Rename option.

Create a Shortcut

You can create a Shortcut on your desktop. Shortcuts are used so that you have easy access to your favorite websites or even your favorite programs you use. To create a shortcut follow these easy steps.

Step 1. Right click anywhere on your desktop.

Step 2. Notice the options menu that popped up. Look for the option that says New.

Step 3. You should have moved your mouse down to the New option,
    A new window
of options should have opened next to the options that are open. Now look for the option that says Shortcut. Click that option.

Step 4. A new window should have opened with a bar you can type your favorite web address in or an option for browse. Here is an example of a web address you can type in, WWW.updates.Microsoft.com you would push next after you entered that and it would ask for a name for the new short cut. The name I would give this example would be Microsoft Updates.

Step 5. To add your favorite program you would press Browse instead of type where you put the web address. Once you found your program you would then follow the rest of Step 4's instructions.

Set your Screen Saver

Here are the steps to setting your screen saver.

Step 1. Right Click anywhere on the desktop.

Step 2. When the little pop up option window appears find the properties option. Click that.

Step 3. The Display Properties Window will open. Look at the different Tabs at the
top of the window. It should have opened in the Themes Tab, now look for
the Tab called Screen Savers. Click that Tab.

Step 4. You are now in the Screen Saver Options. In these options you will be able
to tell your computer how long it has to be idle before the screen saver can
activate and you can choose your screen saver.

Step 5. Once you have set the screen saver to what you want. Select OK so that it
will save your options and exit.

Set your Desktop Background

Windows allows you to choose what you would like your background to be. There are 2 different ways that you can set your Desktop Background. Here are the steps to choosing your Background.

Step 1. If you are on a website and really like a picture and want it as your Desktop
Background here is how you can do that. Right click the picture.
Step 2. A menu option will appear, Look for the option Set as Background or Set as
Desktop Background. Push that.
Step 3. The second way to set a Desktop Background is. Right click anywhere on your Desktop.
Step 4. The option window will appear. Find Properties then Click that.
Step 5. An properties window should have opened. Look at the Tabs at the top. Find the one that say Desktop. Once you have found that push it.
Step 6. You are now in the Desktop Background options. In these options you can choose a pre-loaded desktop Background or choose from the Pictures you have in My Pictures. If you have more pictures some where else you will

have to push the Browse option.

Step 7. Now you can choose from the 3 options on the page for how you want the picture displayed. They are Center, Tile, or Stretch. Choose your option then press OK.

Internet Explorer Content Adviser

You would use this to block sites that you find unsuitable for people to view. This can be used to keep children out of chat sites and even pornographic websites. After you activate the Content Adviser you will be prompted to set an administrator password. This password is so that if you ever want to change settings or view a blocked web page you can override the blocker. Here are the steps to setting it up.

Step 1. Open your Internet Explorer Web Browser.

Step 2. Find the option that says tools. Located at the top.

Step 3. When the tools option opens you will need to find the Internet options link.
Push that.

Step 4. When the Internet Options opens you will see that there are 7 different tabs
at the top. Find the Content Tab and push it.

Step 5. Now that you are in the Content options find the Content Adviser activation
button. Push it.

Step 6. You have now enabled your content adviser. As a default setting everything
is blocked now. To unblock the websites you wish to allow you will need to
go though each of the different content things and move the Bar to the
right. That makes it so you can unblock certain sites.

Step 7. Once you have set the Content you wish to allow you need to press OK.

Step 8. Now you will be asked to create a password and hint. This is so if you wish
to change or shut off the Content Adviser or Allow a website to be viewed
all you will have to do is enter the password.

Virus Protection

In today's day in age virus protection is a must. You can spend a good amount of money on virus protection, but why do that when there is a free on that works real well. Here are the steps in downloading the free virus protection.

Step 1. Go to the web page WWW.avira.com.

Step 2. Once you get on to the web page look on the left of the page for Downloads.

Step 3. OK now you have clicked Downloads. You should see the words Desktop with some links under it. Find the link called "Avira AntiVir Personal- Free Anti Virus." Once you have found that Click the link.

Step 4. A new web page should have opened. Click the Green Download Now Button.

Step 5. That will open up yet again a new web page. Where you will need to click on
the Download now Button again.

Step 6. If a yellow security warning pops down from the top of the web page just under the tab, you need to click it and push the Download now button to begin the download.

Step 7. Now a window should pop up giving you the option to Run or Save the download. If you just want to run the file it will download the needed files so that it can install. If you would like to save the file press save a new window will pop up letting you pick the location to save the file. It is always best to have a folder to were you save all your downloads to, or just save it to your desktop. This is just so you can find the file.

Step 8. Once the file completes downloading click the run button and follow the install directions.

Note: There are other good free Virus programs my favorite is Malwarebytes. WWW.malwarebytes.org is the website just follow the above steps to download.

Configure Avira Anti-virus

This is only if you have downloaded and installed the free Avira Anti-virus.

Step 1. Once the Virus software is installed the main window should pop up. If the
window does not pop up then you need to find the Red umbrella icon and double click it. It may also be in a small icon down by the clock in the right hand corner.

Step 2. Once the main menu is opened make sure all the options in the center of the
screen all have Green checks next to them. If you need to update the virus definitions do so by clicking the start update button on the right side of the screen.

Step 3. To configure the virus scanner to do a system scan at a certain time you need to find the Administration button on the left hand side.

Step 4. Now you have two options after you clicked Administration find the one that says scheduler and click it.

Step 5. To enable the scheduler you need to check the box under enabled.

Step 6. Now you need to right click on the job. A gray window should pop up. Find
where it says edit job and select that.

Step 7. Push next until you get to the Time of Job option. This is were your going to
pick the time you wish the scan to happen and how often it need to scan.

Step 8. Now push next until you get to the Finished Button after you push that your
done.

Repair for the dreaded blue screen of death windows XP

PC users, you all know what it is: That dreaded Blue Screen of Death. That's right, the BSOD. You've installed a seemingly innocent application, restarted your computer, and suddenly you see this horror in front of your eyes: A big blue screen with some cryptic message on it. Try restarting again, same thing. You're dead. What will you do? What WILL you do?? Well, don't let it ruin your day. Remain calm. If you're using Windows XP, I can help you fix it. Come with me, down into the bowels of Windows XP, where only the high priests go. It'll be fun!

I'm going to show you how to bring your computer back to life, and restore it to the point where things went south. You might want to print this article and squirrel it away for that fateful day when this happens to you. Or if you don't want to print it (and who prints anything these days, anyway?), and you get a big ugly blue screen, just get on another computer somewhere and come back to this Web page for comfort and advice. I can get you out of this mess. I know, because I was in the same mess and I got myself out of it.

Here's what to do: First, get the Windows XP CD you used to install your operating system. By the way, this routine only works with Windows XP, either Professional or XP Home Edition. If you don't have a bootable XP CD, get one and have it with you at all times, because you never know when the dreaded BSOD might strike.

But before you do anything with that CD, try restarting your computer again. Sometimes, for some odd reason, this works. Usually not, though. If you've tried that and everything else you can think of, and you can't even boot into Safe Mode, this is the mission for you.

Put the XP CD in the drive, and restart. When it says "press any key to boot from CD," go ahead, press any key and you're on your way to recovery.

Press F6 if you have Raid Drives and later select 'S' and place your Raid driver in the 'A' Drive. Select your Driver for the list and then press Enter. After installation press Enter to continue.

The Recovery Console, that is. If it doesn't give you a choice to boot from your CD drive, go into your computer's BIOS and make the adjustment for it to boot from CD. PCs brands and motherboards are too diverse for me to give you specifics on this, so follow the prompts and you can make that CD boot happen without too much trouble. Look at your screen when it boots up, and it always says "hit DEL for BIOS settings" or something similar. If you can't get it to boot from CD, just give up and call for support or take your computer to the nearest computer store for professional help.

OK, troops, are you still with me? Good. It'll look like you're re-installing Windows XP, but don't worry, you're not. This is just a screen showing you that your computer is loading enough files from the CD to actually do something, anything but that awful blue screen. Now when you see the screen that asks you if you want to install Windows, don't! Just hit R for recover, and you'll see the ominous Recovery Console. Don't let that intimidate you; the Recovery Console is your ugly, black-suited friend. It will have a dark, bleak screen, with the following stuff:

Microsoft Windows(R) Recovery Console

The Recovery Console provides system repair and recovery functionality.
Type EXIT to quit the Recovery Console and restart the computer.

: C:\WINDOWS

Which Windows Installation would you like to log onto
(To cancel, press ENTER)?

Go ahead and hit the number 1 on your keyboard, or whichever number corresponds to the operating system you were using when havoc struck. Enter your administrator password, and then hit enter. You're in! Now it's time to run with the big dogs! Do not be afraid, dear reader, I am here to help you.

If you type the following commands into your computer, it will work magic, akin to going back in time. There are three parts to this process, but believe me, they take much less time than reinstalling Windows XP and all your applications. So follow along with me, and keep in mind that each command must be typed exactly as you see it here. Please note that this procedure assumes that Windows XP is installed to the C:\Windows folder. Make sure to change C:\Windows to the appropriate windows folder if it's at a different location. The copy commands will answer you with a little "file copied" message. The delete commands just move on to the next line. Because of the way your Web browser displays individual lines, a command might look to you like it's two lines, so I've separated each command by an empty line. But anyway, type the whole command in one line, and when you've finished typing that command, hit the Enter key. Be sure to include the spaces I've included between each word here:

md tmp

copy C:\windows\system32\config\system C:\windows\tmp\system.bak

copy C:\windows\system32\config\software C:\windows\tmp\software.bak

copy C:\windows\system32\config\sam C:\windows\tmp\sam.bak

copy C:\windows\system32\config\security C:\windows\tmp\security.bak

copy C:\windows\system32\config\default C:\windows\tmp\default.bak delete C:\windows\system32\config\system

delete C:\windows\system32\config\software

delete C:\windows\system32\config\Sam

delete C:\windows\system32\config\security

delete C:\windows\system32\config\default

copy C:\windows\repair\system C:\windows\system32\config\system

copy C:\windows\repair\software C:\windows\system32\config\software

copy C:\windows\repair\sam C:\windows\system32\config\sam

copy C:\windows\repair\security C:\windows\system32\config\security

copy C:\windows\repair\default C:\windows\system32\config\default

Now you can relax for a minute. You've made it through the first part! Way to go! Now what did you just do? I'll tell you. You first made a temporary directory called "tmp" (md tmp), and then into it, you copied all the files that boot up Windows. Then you deleted all those startup files, one of which is the stinker that got you into this mess in the first place. After that, you copied into that same place fresh startup files from a special repair directory. When you reboot, Windows will look for those files where it always does, and there won't be a stinker in the bunch. The only thing is, there won't be all your settings for all those applications you run every day, either. But not to worry. Right now, you're sitting in something like a lifeboat -- it's not the original ship, but it'll get you back to where you need to go. We'll get everything back to that comfortable place, but only after we go through the next steps.

Now type Exit and watch your computer restart into Windows XP again. Be sure not to tell it to boot from the CD this time. But wait. That's not the way you had XP set up before this disaster struck! That's OK. We're in a lifeboat right now -- this isn't your comfy cruise ship, not just yet. Hang in there. I'm going to show you how to restore your system to the way it was the moment before you told it to install that errant application, or whatever it was you did, so follow along and we'll go to the next step.

Here's where you'll copy the saved registry files from their backed up location by using System Restore. This folder is not available in Recovery Console and is normally not visible -- Microsoft is protecting you from yourself by hiding it from you and locking it away from you. But we have the keys. Before you start this procedure, you'll need to change several settings to make that folder visible:

. Start Windows Explorer.

. On the Tools menu, click Folder options.

. Click the View tab.

. Under Hidden files and folders, click to select Show hidden files and folders, and then click to clear the "Hide protected operating system files (Recommended)" check box.

. Click Yes when the dialog box is displayed that confirms that you want to display these files.

. Double-click the drive where you installed Windows XP to get a list of the folders. It's important to click the correct drive.

. Open the System Volume Information folder. This folder appears dimmed because it is set as a super-hidden folder. If you're using the FAT32 file system, this will be easy. If you're using NTFS, it won't let you open the folder, but here's how to get around that: Right-click on that system volume information folder and select Sharing and Security. Then click the Security tab. (No security tab? Skip two paragraphs.) Click Add, and then in the box that's labeled "Enter the object names to select," type the name of the user that's at the top of the Start menu -- that's probably you. [Damn it, why do they say object names when it's people's names? I guess that's Microsoft for you.]

Anyway, make sure you type the name the way it's listed there on the Start Menu. I made the mistake of typing my first name only and it wouldn't let me in. Type first and last name if that's how it's written on the top of the Start menu. After you've typed that in, click OK a couple of times and finally that monster will let you in.

But what if you don't see a Security tab? Try this: Click to select the checkboxes in the "Network sharing and security" area -- one is labeled "Share this folder on the network" and the other is labeled "Allow network users to change my files." Change the share name to something short, like sysinfo. Then it'll let you in. After you're done with this entire rescue operation, you might want to go back and change these back to the way they were before, for maximum security.

OK. Now here you are, in the inner sanctum where only the high priests go. Be not afraid, all ye who enter here. As Microsoft so eloquently puts it:

NOTE : This folder contains one or more _restore {GUID} folders such as "_restore{87BD3667-3246-476B-923F-F86E30B3E7F8}".

. Open a folder that was not created at the current time. You may have to click Details on the View menu to see when these folders were created. There may be one or more folders starting with "RP x under this folder. These are restore points.

. Open one of these folders to locate a Snapshot subfolder; the following path is an example of a folder path to the Snapshot folder:

C:\System Volume Information_restore{D86480E3-73EF-47BC-A0EB-A81BE6EE3ED8}RP1Snapshot

From the Snapshot folder, copy the following files to the C:\Windows\Tmp folder (you can use your mouse, you're in Windows now, remember?):

_registry_user_.default
_registry_machine_security
_registry_machine_software
_registry_machine_system
_registry_machine_sam

This is how Microsoft explains this: "These files are the backed up registry files from System Restore. Because you used the registry file created by Setup, this registry does not know that these restore points exist and are available. A new folder is created with a new GUID under System Volume Information and a restore point is created that includes a copy of the registry files that were copied during part one. This is why it is important not to use the most current folder, especially if the time stamp on the folder is the same as the current time."

Anyway, you're still not done. Don't worry, the magic is about to begin. Believe me, if you do this in front of your friends, they'll start thinking you're some kind of god. So, heavenly father, get ready to dazzle 'em.

Now it's time to place those files you just made visible to the Recovery Console where they belong. And to do that, we need to get back into the Recovery Console. So, make sure your CD is in the drive, and restart Windows, this time hitting any key when it tells you to do that if you want to boot from CD.

Don't forget to press F6 if you have Raid Driver and load the Raid Driver.

Yes, you want to boot from CD, so you can launch your old cryptic pal, the Recovery Console. Type R after it goes through that file-reading routine that looks like an install but isn't. Then you're back into our dark-suited friend with its ominous command line. It's kinda like going into the basement to fix some broken pipe or something. But we're not scared. The command line is our flashlight and friend. Here we go:

In this part, you delete the existing registry files, and then copy the System Restore Registry files to the C:\Windows\System32\Config folder:

From within Recovery Console, type the following commands:

Del c:\windows\system32\config\sam

Del c:\windows\system32\config\security

Del c:\windows\system32\config\software

Del c:\windows\system32\config\default

Del c:\windows\system32\config\system

copy c:\windows\tmp_registry_machine_software c:\windows\system32\config\software

copy c:\windows\tmp_registry_machine_system c:\windows\system32\config\system

copy c:\windows\tmp_registry_machine_sam c:\windows\system32\config\sam

copy c:\windows\tmp_registry_machine_security c:\windows\system32\config\security

copy c:\windows\tmp_registry_user_.default c:\windows\system32\config\default

Now. You're done! Type exit and your computer will reboot into whichever restore file you chose. Make sure you don't boot to the CD. But wait. If it's not the right one, that's OK, you can now go into your System Restore area and pick a different restore point if you want. There's a whole calendar full of them in there. I bet you didn't know that Windows XP is watching just about every move you make, taking notes all the while. It can restore about any state you had on that machine. And the best part is, even when it's doing all that, it's still 10% faster than Windows 2000 according to our extensive tests here at the Midwest Test Facility. Here's how to get into that restore area if you're not happy with the current restore point:

. Click Start, then click All Programs.

. Click Accessories, and then click System Tools.

. Click System Restore, and then click Restore to a previous Restore Point.

Sheesh, before this I hated the command line. Many of you probably still do. But when it saves your butt like this, you have to feel grateful. I should send out a badge of courage for all you intrepid souls who followed me into these dark gallows, the basement of Windows XP. I hope this routine was successful in bringing your computer back to life. I know how it feels to have your computer down for the count. As a wise old man once told me, "When your computer crashes, it's like your dog just died." He was so right.

Note: I don't know who to give credit to for this information, Just thought I would pass it on.

Windows Defender

Windows Defender is a free program offered by Microsoft. The purpose of this program is to keep your computer safe from spyware. Follow these steps to adding Windows defender to your computer.

Step 1. Go to the Microsoft web site at www.microsoft.com/downloads.
Step 2. You should be in the Microsoft Download Center. Find the search bar that says Bing. Type Windows Defender in the search bar.
Step 3. Now some links should have showed up. Click the link that says Windows Defender link, should be the first one.
Step 4. Now you should see the download button. Click That button.
Step 5. Once the download is complete follow the instructions to install the program.

Microsoft Internet Explorer Pop-Up Blocker

Windows Internet Explorer has a built in Pop-Up Blocker. A Pop-Up Blocker is a program that is used to block them annoying pop-up advertisements that some web sites have. Here are the steps to make sure you Pop-Up Blocker is activated.

Step 1. Open your Windows Internet Browser.
Step 2. Once your Browser is open, look for the tools option at the top of your page. Click that option.
Step 3. You will now notice that a pop down window appears. Move your mouse down to the option that says Pop-Up Blocker.
Step 4. A window should open for the Pop-Up Blocker, now if one of the options says click to turn on your Pop-Up Blocker push that. If the option says to click to turn off your Pop-Up Blocker then your Blocker is running.
Step 5. If you wish you can use the other option and set your own setting for how the Pop-Up Blocker works.

Keyboard shortcuts

Ctrl o pressing both of them keys at the same time opens a web search bar or open a file.

Ctrl f pressing them keys at the same time starts a find for if your on a webpage or document.

Ctrl c Pressing them keys at the same time copies highlighted text.

Ctrl p Pressing them keys at he same time paste the copied text.

Pressing the windows key and the E key will open windows exploder.

If you are using the new windows 8 operating system down were the start menu is on other windows operating systems if you right click it will bring up your basic start menu options.

In windows 8 if your in the App start menu if you start typing it will start a search.

A good website to use if you would like to see screen shots is WWW.chasms.com this website will give you screen shots for all the windows operating systems, Mac operating systems, Ipods, E-Mail Clients, and many other useful information. This is a good place to practice trying to locate things on a computer.

The F key's and there uses

I am sure you have been wondering what are them F key's at the top of my keyboard? I also bet you wonder what they do. Well I am going to give you a description of these key's and some of there most used functions.

F1

- you can use this key in most any program by pushing it and it should open up the help menu.
- This key is also used to open the windows help and support center. To be able to open this you will be pushing two key the windows key and the F1 key. Now to locate the Windows Key take a look at your keyboard, now at the bottom of your keyboard do you see a key that kinda looks like a waving flag? This key should be located next to your ALT key. you would press that Windows Key and the F1 key together to open the help and support center. Now not all computers do you have to push the windows key and the F1 key some computers just pushing the F1 key will open the Help and Support center.
- F1 is also used to open the BIOS. The BIOS can be opened when you are first starting your computer before you get to the windows boot. For an example you just turn on your computer you would then press F1 and it would take you into the BIOS. I would not recommend anyone who does not know what they are doing to go in the BIOS. You could damage your computer if you mess with the wrong settings. Once again this key only works on some computers I have seen computers that use the ESC key to enter BIOS or even the DEL key.

F2

- This key when used in Windows is mostly used to Rename an highlighted icon or file.
- You can also use the F2 key to open a new document in Microsoft Word with using these key CTRL ALT F2. You must press all of them Keys at once for this to work.
- By pushing CTRL F2 in Microsoft Word you will be able to open the Print Preview.

F3

- Using this key you can open the Search menu on Microsoft Windows.

- Using the keys Shift F3 in Microsoft Word you will be able to change the text from uppercase to lowercase. This is good for if you forgot to Capitalize the first letter of the sentence if you press it once it will capitalize the first letter of the word your typing and if you press it twice it will Capitalize the whole word if you do that just do it once more time to put it back to all lowercase letters.

F4

- Lets you repeat the last action preformed. (word 2000 +)
- ALT F4 will close the program currently active in Microsoft Windows.
- CTRL F4 will close the open window within the currant active window in Microsoft Windows.

F5

- Will refresh Windows, Any Internet Browser, and programs running in Windows.
- Opens then find, replace, and goto window in Microsoft Word.
- Starts a slide show in Power Point.

F6

- Moves the cursor to the Address Bar in Web Browsers.
- CTRL SHIFT F6 opens another Microsoft Word Document.

F7

- Commonly used to spell and grammar check a document in Microsoft Programs such as Word, Outlook, Excel, Etc.....
- SHIFT F7 runs a Thesaurus check on highlighted words.
- Turns on Caret browsing in Mozilla Firefox.

F8

- Commonly used to enter Windows Start Up menu, and getting into Safe Mode when first turning on a computer not when windows has started.

F9

- Opens the Measurements tool-bar in Quark 5.0.

F10

- In Microsoft Windows this key activates the menu bar of an open application.
- SHIFT F10 is the same as right clicking on an highlighted Icon, File, or Internet Link.

F11

- Clicking this key will put any Internet Browser in full screen.
- At the start up of your computer with some computer models you can enter System Restore with this key.

F12

- **Opens the Save As window in Microsoft Word.**
- **SHIFT F12 Save a Microsoft Word Document.**
- **CTRL SHIFT F12 prints a Document in Microsoft Word.**